Wolfsong in Georgia

Memoirs of a German Shepherd
Dog Family

Alice Lovejoy Carnahan

Copyright © 2013 Alice Lovejoy Carnahan

Cover photo copyright © 2006 Joyce Quick

All rights reserved.

ISBN: 1492745340
ISBN-13: 978-1492745341

Dedication

This book is dedicated to my husband George, the best Dog Daddy in the world. Without him, there would have been no Wolfsong, and no song in my heart.

Acknowledgments

With thanks

To the dogs: Rajah, Delta, Oscar, Christmas, Alexandra, Misha, and Bonnie.

To dog friends, the best kind: Dixie and Jerry Whitman, Joye and Larry Evans, Judith and Armando Aguilar.

To Linda Bankhead, for her suggestions which made this a better and more positive book.

To friend, first reader, fellow ELM student, and terrific dog mom BB Crowder. BB coined the term "dogoir."

To Lloyd Blackwell, instructor at ELM, the Enrichment of Life Movement in Marietta, Georgia, for his encouragement and advice to keep it short.

To Annel Martin, for encouraging me to write and publish and for introducing me to my editor.

To Josh Langston, for his terrific editing, formatting, cover design, and patience. I could not have a better mentor for the world of publishing.

Contents

Acknowledgments	v
How It Began	1
Life Altering Decisions	7
High Tech and Low Gravity	17
The Name Game	21
Mishas's Second Crisis	27
Puppy Evaluation: She's the One!	31
Intussusception	35
Voodoo Vet	39
Oscar: A Tragedy in Four Months	43
Interlude, After Oscar	49
Mortal Enemies	53
Puppy Kindergarten	57
Ears	61
Triumph!	65
The Hike	69
Sheep!	75
Tales From Tranquility	83

Elbows	91
Bunnies, or Dogs Will be Dogs	97
Teflon Dog	101
Miraculous Red Liquid	107
Dog Friends	111
Neurosurgery	117
The Gift	121
Stem Cell Therapy	127
Explosion!	133
Last Dog Standing	137
Afterword	141
About the Author	143
For More Information	145
Photo Credits	146

Pebbles, Dakota's dam.

Dakota

How It Began

Two happy accidents of geography started my husband George and me on our life with German Shepherd Dogs. Our first dog, a Westie (West Highland White Terrier), had died three years previously at age 15, and we were finally ready to consider getting another dog. Because all Westies look very similar--small and white--we didn't want to get another one, knowing that we would always compare our new companion to Ashton and the next guy would never measure up.

We wanted a big dog this time, and wanted to do obedience training. After much research, and after overcoming George's mother's fears of the breed, we decided on a German Shepherd Dog. One Sunday in the *Atlanta Journal-Constitution*, we saw a dog match (an informal competition in conformation: evaluating a dog's structure, appearance, movement, and temperament-- and/or obedience) advertised. The German Shepherd Dog Club of Atlanta was holding it in a park right around the corner from our home!

We arrived there on a scorching Georgia summer morning, and were effusively greeted by Dixie Whitman, a longstanding lover of German Shepherds who was very active in the club. All around were stunningly beautiful dogs. Because the day was so hot, several of the dogs had been allowed to take shade under cloth-covered tables. Only gradually, as canine heads began peeking out from under the tablecloths, did we realize that there were a lot more animals present than we had realized! By happenstance, we had entered the park in the area where obedience competition was occurring.

Watching cheerful, obedient German Shepherds heel, sit, come, and lie down on command thrilled us with the possibility that someday we, too, could have a beautiful German Shepherd Dog who would obey our every instruction.

Dixie graciously introduced us to her husband, Jerry, as well as to many other club members and their dogs. She invited us to come to a meeting of the German Shepherd Dog Club of Atlanta, and assured us that we did not need to own a dog in order to visit and eventually join. She also introduced us to Joye DeMoss (now Joye Evans), from whom Dixie had acquired her lovely solid black female, Dakota.

Once we all began chatting about GSD's (German Shepherd Dogs) and about where we lived, we were astonished to discover that Joye, Dixie and Jerry, and George and I all lived within a five-mile radius of each other.

We became fast friends with Joye, Dixie, and Jerry, and fell in love with their dogs. Joye had bought a solid black puppy from "Scootie" Sherlock, a maven in the world of GSD's, who helped set up the breeding program for the Monks of New Skete, a religious order in upstate New York. They attained fame when they published the acclaimed book, *How to be Your Dog's Best Friend*.

Scootie also bred dogs of her own, and one of her females produced Caralon Madeka's Glitter whom Joye dubbed Pebbles because she reminded her of her old dog, Rocky. After Pebbles matured and earned her AKC CD (Companion Dog) obedience title as well as hip and elbow certifications from the Orthopedic Foundation for Animals (OFA), Joye bred her to a top show dog, AOE (Award of Excellence) Champion Waltraut's That's Black Jack ROM

(Register of Merit), CD, TC (Temperament Certified). She kept two males from that litter, gorgeous dark black and tans R.C. and Jerry (Charbar's Ray Charles and Charbar's Jerry Lee Lewis, respectively), and placed all the others.

Dixie and Jerry adopted Dakota, a solid black littermate to RC and Jerry. They already had Sierra, a wonderful German-American cross that they had bought a couple of years previously.

We had not known that solid black German Shepherds existed, but soon learned that they not only existed, but were perfectly acceptable in terms of the German Shepherd Dog standard. (There is a written standard for every dog breed recognized by the American Kennel Club; it describes what dogs of the specified breed should look like, their structure, how they should move, and their correct temperament.) Most important to us was the temperament of Joye's and Dixie and Jerry's dogs: it was perfect. Scootie was known for producing beautiful, sweet, and healthy dogs, and Pebbles and Dakota carried on those traits in their own litters.

Joye eventually bred Pebbles twice more, and Joye bred Dakota once. We had fallen in love with their whole family of German Shepherd Dogs. So when Dixie told us that she planned to breed Dakota, we asked if we could obtain one of the puppies from that breeding. We told her we wanted a male; we had never had a female, and had no interest whatsoever in breeding dogs ourselves. We just wanted one perfect family companion.

How little we knew....

~*~

Alice Lovejoy Carnahan

Rajah entered our lives, and nothing was ever quite the same.

Life Altering Decisions

A one hundred pound black and tan dog changed our plans and our lives forever. Determined to learn as much as we could about the breed we had chosen, George and I faithfully attended meetings of the German Shepherd Dog Club of Atlanta. We even went, *sans* dog, to dog training classes sponsored by the club and held at a nearby parking garage.

One wonderful Tuesday night Landen Gailey, a GSD Club of Atlanta volunteer instructor and co-founder of the Atlanta German Shepherd Rescue group, handed me a leash, saying the dog on the other end just needed some affection and she knew I would enjoy borrowing him for the class period. Landen had rescued him from the DeKalb County Animal Control Shelter just that morning after getting a call from Suzanne

Kinman, a club member who worked there. No one knew his name, so Landen had dubbed him "Orphan."

He was enormous! (We weighed him later, and he topped out at 102 pounds.) He had a grey muzzle, soulful eyes, and a perfectly straight topline. I thought he was pretty, but it was hard to tell under the sodium vapor glow of the parking garage lights. What I could tell, though, hooked me: he walked on a loose lead, buckle collar, for 60 minutes among strange vans holding strange dogs barking at him, around classes of unknown people and dogs, and he always walked calmly and with confidence, only occasionally glancing up at me with those gorgeous brown eyes if a particularly loud beastie sounded off. George was assisting with a class. When it was over I took Orphan to meet him. George bent his knees a bit (he's six-two), and the dog buried his muzzle in George's belly. I was in love with the dog, and the dog was in love with George. I had to have him. George wailed, "But what about my puppy?" I agreed on the spot to a two-dog household if I could just have this one.

Suzanne told us that he was within 15 minutes of being euthanized when she spotted him; his time had run out. He looked so much like one of her dogs from a great old Atlanta sire that she called German Shepherd Rescue despite his age, estimated at between five and eight. A family in Decatur had turned him in after finding him wandering loose. He lasted a week with them; he probably ate them out of house and home. We eventually got him down to a svelte 85 pounds, but it was a constant battle.

We deliberated over what to name him. While we had our back yard fenced, Orphan stayed in foster care and was called King. But Landen said he responded well to "R" sounds. Royal though he was, "King" was just too common. So he became Karma's Grand Rajah, in honor of the kind fates which had saved his life and brought us together.

Our dog friends told us about a special type of AKC registration available to purebred neutered or spayed dogs. It allows dogs to compete in obedience and other performance events on an equal basis with all other dogs-- no pedigree known or required. Rajah earned his CD title, his Canine Good Citizen™ certification, his Herding Instinct certification, and therapy dog certification. Although he was truly George's dog, Rajah graciously allowed me to take him on hundreds of therapy dog visits to local senior centers and the stroke unit at our local hospital. One night while there, a sweet little patient who usually hummed or sang, while brushing Rajah with his special soft brush said quite clearly, "Good Dog!" Every staff member within hearing distance stopped and stared. Those were the first words the lady had spoken since she had been admitted.

In 1997, Rajah was honored by the American German Shepherd Rescue Association at the German Shepherd Dog Club of America's National specialty show, held in Perry, Georgia, that year. George proudly took Rajah into the huge ring for the presentation, while I sat in the stands and cried tears of joy and pride.

But what about our "perfect puppy?" Rajah derailed those plans, too. We had planned to get a male puppy, but one of our trainers noticed that Rajah, although perfectly behaved in almost all circumstances, was a naturally dominant male and would probably get along better with a female than a male puppy.

We broke the news to Dixie, who was not happy, and understandably so. We had told her for months that we wanted a boy. After Dakota had earned her CD title and obtained hip and elbow certifications, Dixie bred her to top show dog Select Champion Scharo's Spellbinder TC, HIC (Herding Instinct Certified), ROM. Dakota produced seven wonderful puppies, five males and two females. Dixie needed to find perfect homes for all the boys she and Jerry didn't plan to keep, and she had thought that one would go to us. Dixie also knew that we wanted only a pet, and planned to spay our girl puppy. At that time we were still novices and did not fully understand how well-bred those puppies were, and how important it would be to continue their line if at all possible. But we really wanted that puppy!

Because Spellbinder's call name (informal name which a dog goes by) was Magic, Dixie included "Magic" in all her pups' registered names. Delta, the puppy George and I wanted, was Rising Wolf's Delta Magic. Her one female littermate, Katie, was admittedly much better looking, but she was already Jerry's girl. She was dark black and tan, but not as dark as Delta, and she had a very fluffy coat. Delta had what an acquaintance erroneously called a "skin coat," which was more accurately described as close coated. Her coat was thick but very, very close to her body, just the opposite of plush. And she was scrawny, all legs and ears. But when we visited, Delta, although never a lap puppy, would lie down as close as she could get to my thigh while I sat on the floor admiring and playing with the rest of the litter.

George already had "his" dog, Rajah. I wanted a dog of my own. I had to have Delta! So, eventually we agreed that we would not spay Delta until after she had had all of her own health tests, and if she passed all of them (and also earned her own obedience title and CGC certification), we would *consider* breeding her. To Dixie's credit, there was no mention of breeding Delta in the puppy contract. Dixie let us take her home when she was just over nine weeks old.

It was almost a year after Rajah came to grace our home when Delta joined us. She was all we ever dreamed of--and more. She and Rajah gradually became best friends. She was his perfect complement: play-driven, active, and exuberant to his old, calm wisdom. But in her confidence and affectionate nature we like to think we saw not only the product of her superb breeding but also a bit of Rajah's influence as well: a generous heart and a kind and kindred spirit.

She did become "my" dog. We began puppy kindergarten classes two nights after George and I brought her home, and we trained constantly for the next two years. She earned her CD title, as well as her temperament, herding instinct, and Canine Good Citizen™ certifications. Through the dog club's education programs, we learned not only about OFA certifications for hips and elbows, but also about von Willebrand's disease and testing, CERF (Canine Eye Registration Foundation) testing for eyes, tests for pancreatic function, and OFA cardiac and thyroid testing. We decided to test her for everything available at the time. She passed with flying colors.

Dixie, Joye, and Jerry helped educate us about their dogs and our bloodline. By the time we decided we would indeed breed Delta, we said that the three couples were "related through our dogs," which was true: Pebbles had begat RC, Jerry, and Dakota, who then had our Delta and her littermates, Dixie and Jerry's Orly, Cajun, and Katie. They were all beautiful (well, except for Delta who remained all legs and ears until after she had her babies and her chest dropped, when she became quite pretty) and they all were completely trustworthy with people. None of us had human children; the dogs were our "kids."

As much research as we had put into getting the perfect puppy, we put even more into finding the perfect sire for our puppies. By the time we made the decision to breed Delta, Joye had bred Pebbles to Select Champion Winning Ways Chimo, a gorgeous Canadian show dog who had top titles in both Canada and the United States. She had kept two dogs from that litter, Danny and Goldie (no, Goldie was not gold, she was solid black; Joye has a wry sense of humor about naming her dogs). They had just turned two, and she had had their hips and elbows X-rayed. She called with the news that all their joints seemed fine. That clinched the decision for us, because Chimo himself had certifications for good hips and elbows; sound heart and thyroid; he was negative (which is what you want) for von Willebrand's disease, a bleeding disorder; he had good pancreatic function, an indicator of digestive health; he even had OFA certified patellas (knees)!

    It was a fateful choice.

~*~

Wolfsong in Georgia

Delta, a wonderful dog but not a very good reader.

High Tech and Low Gravity

Chimo's chilled semen shipped from Buffalo, New York, to Atlanta, Georgia, via air freight. The service, called "Delta Dash," seemed particularly apt because like the airline, our GSD bride-to-be was named Delta. We refused to fly a dog, and thus had no options other than artificial insemination. Chimo's owners lived just over the border in Canada and graciously volunteered to drive him to Buffalo for the collection.

So on an early February day in 1998, George and I took Delta to the airport, picked up "the box," and then drove to the office of reproductive veterinary specialist Rebecca Kestle, DVM. We were nervous about negotiating Atlanta's interstate highways from the airport to Dr. Kestle's office, excited about the possibility that the breeding might succeed, and exhausted from the many trips and tests we had already made in order to determine exactly the right days to do the breeding. After what seemed like forever, we reached Dr. Kestle's office where she checked the semen sample, declared it of superb quality, inserted it into Delta with a very long pipette, and then instructed me to take Delta into the lobby and hold her hind end up in the air for twenty minutes. I'm sure we made a bizarre wheelbarrow silhouette. Although Delta looked over her shoulder at me as if to ask, "Mom, this is pretty strange, isn't it?" she cooperated without complaint, as she always did.

 Two days later, we repeated the trip and the same combination of high tech and low gravity.

 Then we waited.

 Three weeks after the insemination, our vet palpated Delta but could not tell if she was pregnant. We scheduled an ultrasound appointment with Dr. Kestle for four weeks after the artificial insemination.

 Time crept by. Dixie and Joye must have been beyond annoyed at our constant queries, but they never complained. After all, the puppies would be theirs, too; I had obtained their solemn promise that they would both be present at the whelping, to help. Did they think Delta was pregnant or not? (How would they know?) My colleagues at work, not dog people at all, indulged my all too graphic descriptions of our efforts to have puppies. Finally it was time for the appointment with Dr. Kestle.

Dr. Kestle found "at least seven" puppies! I screamed with joy and hugged Delta, George, and Dr. Kestle in my excitement. After all the tests, all the efforts, all the doubts, it was really true! Delta (and thus we) really were going to have puppies! And seven! We would have been happy with just two or three. (We didn't realize at the time that GSD's can and sometimes do have litters of up to fourteen.) Dr. Kestle offered to shave Delta's belly in order to get an exact count, but in our elation at the news that our first litter was on its way, we declined.

It was a decision we would regret.

Alice Lovejoy Carnahan

Delta and pups.

The Name Game

I wanted perfect names for the perfect puppies we expected, appellations signifying beauty, grace, and athleticism. I decided on classical dancers. I felt strongly that the pups' "call names" should easily relate to their registered names. At too many dog shows I had no idea who the dog being cheered on was, because the call name had no connection to the name in the catalog. We advertised Delta's upcoming litter as "Delta's Dancers." Delta's registered name was Rising Wolf's Delta Magic, so we decided our kennel name would be Wolfsong.

Because all GSD puppies are born extremely dark and look very similar, many breeders put rickrack ribbon collars on the newborns to facilitate identification during the first few weeks. I had chosen many different colors, and had them all readily at hand.

Also ready were Dixie and Joye, who had agreed to help whelp the litter. It was early afternoon, April 1, 1998 (Yes, April Fool's Day). Delta was restless and pacing but refused to settle into the carefully prepared whelping box. Finally I realized that she wanted her special, expensive, orthopedic foam dog bed. I decided to sacrifice it in order to get on with the whelping. It worked; Delta sighed, lay down, and began the business of having puppies.

The first pup was a solid black female. Joye mentioned Pearl Bailey, and the name stuck: she became Pearl. Eventually her registered name would be Wolfsong's Pearl Giselle. Next was a bicolor girl (all black but with tan paws, coloring the same as a Doberman or Rottweiler); the rickrack collar she got was sparkly red, green, and gold. She became Wolfsong's Christmas Pavlova. Third was a bicolor male. He got red rickrack, but no name yet. Next to arrive was a solid black girl, soon fitted with a blue collar. She became "Bonnie Blue," or officially Wolfsong's Bonnie Isadora.

By then, many hours had passed, and Delta was exhausted; so were we. Despite Delta's fatigue, however, she proved an excellent instinctual mom, cleaning the pups, chewing their cords, eating the sacs, and nudging them toward her milk-laden nipples. After a long interval, another bicolor girl arrived. I said that I felt like Prissy in *Gone with the Wind*, because "I don't know nothin' 'bout birthin' no babies!" and voila: this pup was anointed Prissy, whose registered name was to be Wolfsong's Margot Fonteyn.

Next, after another very long interval, Delta pushed out another solid black girl, who soon sported purple rickrack. In our early-morning punchiness (by now it was April 2) we dubbed her "Dr. Lugar," for our veterinarian at the time. Her registered name was Wolfsong Alexandra Danilova, and for a few weeks we tried calling her Xandra, but that didn't take; eventually we called her Alexandra, or Alex for short. In later years George would call her for dinner by proclaiming her sovereignty: "Alexandra Danilova, Princess of All the Russias!"

More hours passed. Dixie briefly napped while Joye and I stayed with Delta. George, awake but sleepy, stayed nearby. I was disappointed that so far we had only one male. We had planned to keep one boy for sure, and possibly also one girl. According to Joye and Dixie, our lines normally produced a preponderance of males in every litter, so we thought we would have plenty of boys to choose from. Eventually, as though in answer to our prayers, out came a little black and tan male. But there was a problem: he had no sac and was not breathing. Dixie, roused by me, came to the rescue, slinging him round while sandwiching his tiny body with two hands, supporting him, and blowing into his mouth. She was a former vet assistant and knew what to try. After what seemed a very, very long time, he began to breathe. I think George and I knew then that this little boy would never leave our home.

    Because there were just the two males, we began joking about "The Odd Couple," and the males were christened Oscar (the bicolor) and Felix, the little black and tan boy. (Unlike solid black and bicolor GSD's, black and tans lighten as they get older, although it was clear at his birth that this boy would become a very dark black and tan, much darker than the traditional "Rin Tin Tin" coloring of tan with just a black saddle.) Oscar was to have been Wolfsong's Rudolf Nureyev, and the other male would be officially registered as Wolfsong's Misha Baryshnikov, the only pup to have the exact appellation I had chosen long before his birth. But for now, the names Oscar and Felix stuck.

Delta did at last have one more pup, number eight, who was stillborn. Joye wrapped her in a towel and told us it was another little black girl. George buried her in the front yard. Had we asked Dr. Kestle to shave Delta to obtain an exact puppy count, we might have been able to intervene earlier; the black and tan boy might not have had the myriad of difficulties at birth and throughout his life, and perhaps orange ribbon, as we called the stillborn, could have survived.

A few weeks later, George asked if we could name "Felix" Misha, as that sounded like "mouse," and with his skinny black body and quizzical tan eyebrows, the pup reminded George of a little mouse. And so Felix became Misha.

Each of these puppies had a unique existence. They brought us joy, tragedy, heartache, and triumph.

These are stories from their lives.

~*~

Alice Lovejoy Carnahan

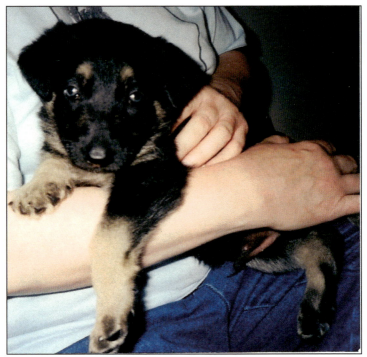

Our little Misha.

Misha's Second Crisis

When all the other pups got up and started walking at around three weeks of age, Misha didn't. Because he still had to crawl to get to Delta, he got less milk than his littermates. We had no idea what was wrong, and feared that he had some horrible residual issues from his whelping, so we wrapped him carefully and took him to Dr. Lugar. He made such a tiny bundle. She examined him, diagnosed a ruptured cruciate ligament, and referred us to Dr. Tom Early for surgery.

Dr. Early worked in the building which also housed the Cobb Emergency Veterinary clinic. After checking over our little pup, he said, "Misha does *not* have a ruptured cruciate ligament, but he does have a luxated patella (kneecap). The good news is that he does not need surgery. I confess, I've never seen a luxated patella--which causes the knee to slip out of place--in a large dog, although it is very common in small breeds."

Trying to be completely honest, he told us his efforts to treat Misha would amount to on-the-job training. He fashioned a sling for Misha's tiny left rear leg, to try to keep the knee in place. One of the many ironies of this breeding was that Misha's sire, Chimo, in addition to having certifications for good hips, elbows, heart, thyroid, eyes, and pancreatic function, also was certified for having good patellas. It was the only certification Chimo had that Delta did not. We never had her tested for patella problems because we had never heard of any GSD with slipping knees. Delta's knees were fine throughout her long, healthy life. Another irony, which came to light only later, was that when Dr. Early palpated Misha's little puppy hips, he said they both felt just fine.

Unfortunately the sling, which was flexible, frequently got out of position, pulling Misha's leg forward. When Dixie visited a few days later, she looked at it and suspected it was doing more harm than good. George, who worked at home, took Misha back to Dr. Early. This time he made a rigid sling which did eventually enable Misha to walk.

Unbeknownst to us, however, grave damage had already been done.

Wolfsong in Georgia

~*~

Alice Lovejoy Carnahan

Christmas with Rajah -- she's the one!

Puppy Evaluation: She's the One!

Atlanta is a hot bed of nationally and internationally respected dog show judges as well as top breeders, conformation, and performance competitors. When our puppies were seven weeks old, Dr. Don Jones, whom we had met at the Atlanta Kennel Club and who would go on to judge Best in Show at Westminster in 2008, graciously agreed to evaluate them. We had bred first for health and temperament, but planned to show in conformation if any of our babies had the structure and movement required by the German Shepherd Dog standard. All of the males in our pedigree were top German Shepherd show dogs, and all of the females had at least one obedience title. Dr. Jones (whom everyone just called Don) came to our home to give his objective and very educated opinion of the puppies.

Misha did not participate because he was still in his sling.

Don watched all the other puppies move off leash one at a time while George and I called them back and forth. It did not take him long: he chose Christmas and Bonnie as the best two show prospects.

I asked him if one was better than the other, and he said, "Oh yes, that one," pointing to Christmas. "She has presence."

Wolfsong in Georgia

Skinny Christmas -- no fat, all heart.

Intussusception

Misha's treatment continued through the spring. When he and his littermates were eight weeks old and had had their first set of puppy shots, Misha developed horrible diarrhea. By the next day, all the others had it, too. We immediately took them to Dr. Lugar, who treated them with intensive intravenous antibiotics and kept them at her clinic for a few days. She said, "It looks like parvo and smells like parvo," but the test results did not confirm that diagnosis. It could have been coronavirus, or might have actually been parvo, as testing for that condition at the time was not always accurate. Fortunately, all of the puppies except Christmas recovered completely. We never knew for sure what the virus was, but we believe that Misha probably picked it up in the Emergency Clinic building, where very ill dogs are brought--some with airborne diseases--during one of his trips there.

Dr. Lugar offered to take Christmas home with her and we agreed. I was still working full time in downtown Atlanta, so George, who worked from home, visited Christmas often. On one Monday he came home and said the pup acted as though "she's not our Christmas." It turned out that George, who knew our sweet, feisty, bicolor girl better than anyone else, was the most astute observer. It was not until Wednesday that Dr. Lugar called and referred us to a specialist, as Christmas had declined rather than improving.

Christmas's intestines were literally spilling out of her rear as she was taken for an ultrasound. It showed that she had either a blockage or an *intussusception*, a word we had never heard before. She went to the emergency clinic for exploratory surgery. The veterinarian on call, to his immense credit, reported after his initial exploration that the rest of the needed surgery would be so potentially dangerous that he would like to call in "the best veterinary surgeon in Georgia." That surgeon was Dr. Early.

Christmas did have an intussusception, triggered by severe diarrhea which caused her intestines to telescope into one another and die. It occurs in human babies as well. No one knows why acute diarrhea causes it in some individuals and not in others. The only cure is to remove all the necrotic tissue and patch up what is left. We later said that Christmas had guts, but only of the metaphorical kind--her real ones were mostly removed when she was nine weeks old. Dr. Early said that the intussusception had probably begun two or three days before, just when George had said, "she doesn't act like our little Christmas."

Because Christmas would need a blood transfusion, George went home and brought Delta back. She donated blood for her daughter, taken from her jugular vein, without a flinch. Dixie brought us all a bottle of Rescue Remedy, an herbal supplement used to calm people and animals in times of crisis. Emergency Clinic staff graciously gave us the use of a small private room after Christmas was rushed off for her operation. Dr. Lugar visited, bringing pizza for everyone. Joye came for support. Hours passed. Finally Dr. Early came to give us the news: the operation was a success.

He had saved our little girl's life.

~*~

Misha beats the odds with the Voodoo Vet.

Voodoo Vet

We were overjoyed when the rigid sling that Dr. Early had made for Misha enabled him to walk on his own. However, unknown to any of us, the first sling had already done permanent damage: it had pulled Misha's left hip out of its socket. Very young puppies, like human babies, are still quite "plastic." Their little joints are not yet set, and can easily be disturbed.

So it soon became obvious that although Misha could now walk, he was very, very lame. We had heard of Loving Touch holistic veterinary practice from friends in the German Shepherd Dog Club of Atlanta, and we had taken Rajah, our first shepherd, there. Dr. Michelle Tilghman was and is an internationally famous holistic practitioner.

After one acupuncture treatment, the elderly Rajah came home running like a puppy.

Dr. Tilghman, or "Dr. Michelle" as everyone calls her, evaluated Misha and had an astounding suggestion: gold bead implants at acupuncture points. We conferred with our friend Diane Castle, a vet, who said she didn't think it would hurt, and we could always have a hip replacement done later if it didn't work. (That turned out to be incorrect; Diane had no way of knowing that Misha's hip had been pulled so far out of its socket that the socket was too shallow for a hip replacement to fit.)

Dr. Michelle told us that in Scandinavia, gold bead implants were the first line of treatment for dogs with hip dysplasia. The vet who had pioneered their use in the United States was coming to her clinic to implant them in several of her patients. We wasted no time scheduling Misha. The procedure would be done under very light anesthesia, and would not require him to stay at the clinic overnight.

Such an unusual treatment approach would never have been my first choice. I come from a family which considered all alternate practitioners to be frauds. George's and my willingness to consider taking our poor little boy to what sounded like a "voodoo vet" for such a bizarre sounding treatment was a measure of our desperation to help him.

He had the procedure. Three tiny gold beads were implanted at acupressure points in his left hip. He came home and started running for the first time in his young life. Although there were many crises along the way, he ran for virtually the rest of his life.

Our beautiful little black and tan boy with the quizzical tan eyebrows had been saved by the voodoo vet.

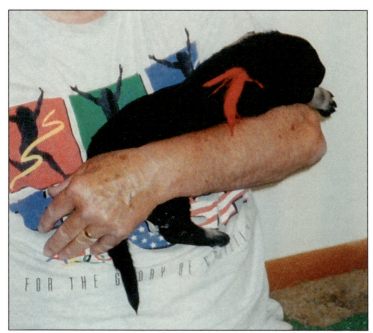

Oscar.

Alice Lovejoy Carnahan

Oscar: A Tragedy in Four Months

He was a chunk, stocky and all black except for his tan paws, with a blocky face and ears that came up early and perfectly straight. He had tremendous bone and even as a youngster in his red puppy collar he had the pulling power of a draft horse. Like his brother Misha, he was over-angulated with a very long upper rear leg, which gave him a long, ground-covering gait. His registered name was to be Wolfsong's Rudolf Nureyev.

Because Delta had chewed off his umbilical cord too close to his body, he had a large umbilical hernia that would have to be surgically repaired. We had to wait until he was three months old. Meanwhile, he loved to lie next to George in the back yard and chew on pine cones. His hernia probably hurt him, and the chewing provided a distraction. And, of course, next to George was the best possible place to be.

By the time Oscar had his surgery, Christmas had already had her intussusception repaired, and Misha had weathered his luxated patella crisis. We knew we would keep Christmas, Bonnie, and Misha, but we had planned to place the others. Pearl was the first to go. It was wrenching, and we never felt quite right about it. When she was placed in her new owner's car, she looked at us as though we were betraying her. We had sold her on a six-month payment plan, believing that it would be better for her to go on to a home of her own than for us to get all of her purchase price up front.

Still, we planned to place Alexandra, Prissy, and Oscar. We had originally planned to keep only one boy and one girl, but after Misha and Christmas's medical problems, we knew we needed to keep both of them. Bonnie was the second pick of the litter, and at that time we thought we might eventually breed her.

One evening we got a call from a responsible-sounding gentleman who had been referred to us by Dr. Carmen Battaglia, a world-renowned judge and breeder whom we had met through the German Shepherd Dog Club of Atlanta. Carmen knew we were very concerned about breeding for the best possible health, and he kindly referred this potential puppy buyer to us.

Mr. X, as I'll call him, told a bizarre story: he had a son and a daughter, and recently his wife had left them all, taking only their beloved German Shepherd Dog with her.

They lived in an upscale neighborhood in metro Atlanta, with a fenced yard and a swimming pool. Although the swimming pool itself was not fenced, he assured us that their dog had never had unsupervised access to it and neither would a puppy. After a long visit during which the children had a wonderful time playing with the pups, Mr. X asked us if we would consider letting them have two puppies, one for each child.

George and I consulted privately, and decided that Prissy and Oscar should do fine together. However, Oscar had not yet recovered from his surgery, so his new family would have to wait a week to pick up their new canine charges.

Oscar had his stitches out and was happy and pain-free, possibly for the first time in his short life. In a week, as scheduled, his new family came to pick him and Prissy up. They made a stunning pair, both bicolor, shining ebony with tan paws.

Mr. X called in a few days to ask about their worming schedule, which we gladly gave him. Then, exactly one week after we had placed Prissy and Oscar, he called to tell us that Oscar was dead. He had dug out from his pen, got into the swimming pool and drowned. He was exactly four months old.

Wolfsong in Georgia

Alice Lovejoy Carnahan

The Rainbow Bridge

There is a bridge connecting Heaven and Earth. It is called the Rainbow Bridge because of its many colors. Just this side of the Rainbow Bridge there is a land of meadows, hills and valleys with lush green grass. When a beloved pet dies, the pet goes to this place. There is always food and water and warm spring weather. The old and frail animals are young again. Those who are maimed are made whole again. They play all day with each other.

There is only one thing missing. They are not with their special person who loved them on Earth. So each day they run and play until the day comes when one suddenly stops playing and looks up!

The nose twitches! The ears are up! The eyes are staring! And this one suddenly runs from the group! You have been seen, and when you and your special friend meet, you take him or her in your arms and embrace. Your face is kissed again and again and again, and you look once more into the eyes of your trusting pet.

Then you cross the Rainbow Bridge together...

— Author Unknown

Interlude, After Oscar

The week before Oscar died, my mother had been diagnosed with dementia. She also had severe osteoarthritis, could not walk without assistance, and had in-home caregivers, when they showed up. My sister Lynne and I tried valiantly to help her remain in her own home, her fervent wish. Despite our best efforts, she was unable to stay at home, and after yet another hospitalization, we placed her in the nicest Assisted Living home we could find.

There had also been the stress of caring for the puppies, including the two with serious medical problems, and of trying to find perfect homes for the ones we planned to place. George shouldered most of the burden of puppy care while I worked away from home and shuttled back and forth from my job to my mother's house to the hospital. When I heard that Oscar was dead, I went crazy. The politically correct term for it was clinical depression, but crazy was how it *felt*. George, who had suffered severe depression his entire life and had family problems far beyond mine, rose above his own problems to help me. After a few months with his comfort, along with the antidepressant drug Zoloft, I began once again to care about life.

    Mr. X had called a couple of weeks after Oscar's death to ask if we knew of a good breeder, as he wanted to get another puppy for the child who had lost Oscar. I was too fragile to talk with him for long, but I referred him to Gail and Hank Cobleigh, very successful and responsible breeders. I also referred him to Joye, who had a long conversation with him and then tried to assuage my guilt over placing Oscar in a home with an unfenced pool. I later ran into Hank at a dog club meeting, and he told me he and Gail had placed a puppy with Mr. X and his family, and that they now had a fence around the pool as well as an alarm system. I hope Prissy benefitted from that. I could never bring myself to contact him to ask about her. My prayer is that she had a long and happy life.

    Shortly after we lost Oscar, George said, "We're not going to place any more puppies." I readily agreed. Thus, Alexandra became a permanent part of our group and went on to become the love of George's life. She joined Delta, Christmas, Bonnie, Misha, George and me as we became the Wolfsong family.

**Alex, Bonnie and Christmas, before the bad blood.
Note Misha in the background behind the crate.**

Mortal Enemies

Shortly after she survived the intussusception surgery, Christmas became very ill. We took her to the University of Georgia's veterinary school, where the staff treated her royally. We visited often. After many weeks, she was well enough to come home.

At that time we didn't know if whatever she had (a bacterial overgrowth; no one was ever able to identify exactly what strains of bacteria) might be contagious to her littermates. So, for several months she lived in an indoor kennel in our home. George almost killed himself taking care of her and her kennel, cleaning it at least once an *hour*, night and day. Eventually we got the okay to let her be with her siblings.

George saw it happen. Bonnie came up to Christmas and lowered her head, a classic gesture of submission. Instead of acknowledging it, Christmas bit Bonnie just above her eye. Bonnie, incensed, went after Christmas with hatred in her heart. Because Christmas was so scrawny, Bonnie savaged her. We had to take Christmas for stitches--the first of many times--until we finally gave up and separated Christmas and Bonnie permanently.

Christmas was only nine weeks old when she had her surgery, and she had been separated from her dam and littermates for months after that. She had lost all of her doggy social skills, and no longer knew how to act around other dogs.

She was naturally dominant and self-confident. Bonnie was naturally insecure. Delta, their dam, didn't know she was a dog and got along with everyone, canine and human. I think she thought she was my sister. Misha took great joy in trying to boss the girls around--except for Christmas, who thought he was her boy toy. She would roar up to him and leap upon his withers with her tiny tan paws, snarling with excitement. He did not share her enthusiasm.

Christmas and Delta were able to live together. When we moved to a new home to accommodate our pack, Christmas and Delta lived on the main level with George and me, with dog door access to their very own paddock. Alex, Bonnie, and Misha lived in the finished basement and had a larger paddock, also with a dog door. It was a good situation for all of us and kept us from having to rotate dogs several times a day, which we had been required to do in the old house.

 Alex, unlike Bonnie, was completely sure of herself. Once when George and I were taking obedience and agility classes, Christmas got loose from me, ran to Alex, and leaped upon her. Alex just turned her head as though to say, "You silly creature; responding to your crazy behavior is far beneath me." Nevertheless, we never allowed Christmas and Alex to live together.

 As for Bonnie, she never forgave Christmas, and they were mortal enemies for the rest of their lives.

Misha, smiling.

Puppy Kindergarten

All dogs need basic manners. Big dogs must be trained from a very young age to behave appropriately. If you don't train them, they will most certainly train you! Puppy kindergarten is perfect for young pups. They may start any time after their second set of shots.

Our local GSD Club was not offering puppy kindergarten when we needed it, so we did training at home and also found a place in Decatur where we could take them.

At home in the back yard, George began teaching the pups to sit for a cookie. Armed with a bag of treats, he sat on a park bench and called their names one by one. When each sat for the "cookie," earning it immediately, George moved to the next pup. They would end up in a perfect row of cute little GSD puppies sitting expectantly before him. He called them in the same order each time: Alex, Christmas, Bonnie, Misha. Alex, Christmas, Bonnie, Misha. They had already learned how to sit for a cookie, and now they learned to associate their names with sitting and getting a treat, and how to wait. Except that Misha--cuddly little Misha who we worried might have brain damage from his traumatic birth--one day got up from the end of the row and plopped himself at the head of the line. Instant promotion! We decided he didn't have brain damage after all.

When we finally got him and some of his siblings to puppy kindergarten classes in Decatur, it was a bust because they were the only puppies there--so much for learning to socialize with other dogs. But it was not a loss for Misha! The training room had apparently once been a ballet studio, and was lined with floor to ceiling mirrors. Misha went straight to the mirror, gave a doggy smile, and began admiring his image. He would cock his head first one way and then the other. He seemed to be saying, "What a beautiful, cute, and charming boy I am!"

Unlike his siblings, Misha never had any formal training, and never earned any titles or awards. But he had plenty of brainpower.

~*~

Wolfsong in Georgia

Delta with the infamous ear, Santa, and Rajah.

Ears

What, more than anything else, gives a German Shepherd Dog his distinctive appearance? First and foremost, his unmistakable head topped by perfectly vertical, erect ears. But GSD pups are not born with upright ears. If you are lucky, they come up early on their own. If you are not lucky, they are late coming up, or they need help. Such was the case with two of our pups: Misha and Bonnie. German Shepherd Dog ears are *never* cropped; it's a disqualifying fault. But hanging ears are also a disqualifying fault, and besides that, no dog with hanging ears, regardless of pedigree, looks like a true German Shepherd Dog.

So, when Misha and Bonnie's ears were still not completely up by four months (Alex and Christmas's ears were), we asked our friend Gene Valentine--who knows how to do everything with dogs, and do it well--to tape them. Misha stayed home with us and the other pups, but as Bonnie was more active, we boarded her for a few days while the ears "set" under the tape. Misha's ears turned out perfectly, but Bonnie's for some reason turned a bit inward, and for the rest of her life, one of her ears remained slightly "bonneted" when she was at ease. Fortunately, when she was away from home and interested in her surroundings, both of her ears went straight up.

Misha eventually lost a small bit of one ear one night when he went too far with teasing Alexandra, and she put him in his place. The vet at the Emergency Clinic--naturally, this happened on a weekend--said Misha would look as though he had been in a fight but won it.

And yet Delta provided the best ear story. As a pup, she was all ears and legs, and her huge ears must have been very heavy. We took her and Rajah to have their photos made with Santa, and while one of Delta's ears went straight up, the other still folded about half way down. I was almost frantic with worry at the time, but now that is one of our most cherished pictures.

Delta's breeder, Dixie, agreed that something had to be done about Delta's ears. She had heard about a new contraption and agreed to put it on Delta. A couple of popsicle-type sticks were placed inside Delta's ears, and a very thin wire ran above her head, connecting the sticks. There was nothing cruel about it, and it was supposed to work after a week or so.

But a couple of days after we had the ear contraption installed, I heard a scream coming from the living room. Delta had been there keeping George company. He was in his comfortable recliner. Somehow she had got the wire over the recliner's lever, and then had pulled back. I think the scream I heard was a combination of Delta *and* George; I'm not sure which one was louder. I called Dixie and begged her to come immediately to take off the device--we would not take a chance that Delta could hurt herself again.

Dixie, who lived nearby at the time, raced over and removed the sticks and wire. Delta's big, beautiful ears came up right then, and stayed straight up for the rest of her long life.

~*~

Christmas with Dr. Michelle, her favorite holistic vet.

Triumph!

Linda Bankhead, a seasoned dog handler and veteran of countless competitions, watched Christmas as she bounded out of the van. That's all the time it took for Linda to reach a conclusion about our girl's suitability for the ring.

"She's clean coming and going, but she's not pretty and fluffy enough for the all-breed judges, and she's not extreme enough for the specialty ring."

We'd been around dog folk long enough to understand what she meant: Christmas moved correctly according to the German Shepherd Dog standard, both trotting away from and back to an observer. She was moderately built and did not have the extreme length of upper rear leg that gives some shepherds their extremely sloping backs and very outreaching gait.

Linda's honesty came as a breath of fresh air. Many handlers would have gilded the lily in order to line their own pockets. "She could probably win at small shows but will have a very difficult time winning majors," Linda said, "and you could end up spending a lot of money with no championship."

We'd had our doubts about Christmas actually winning large shows and admitted as much. But we asked Linda if she would show her for us at some local shows anyway just for the sake of our vanity, and she agreed.

And thus it was that Christmas, not yet two years old, was entered both weekend days in a large Open class at Atlanta's Jonesboro Road Expo Center. Saturday was a disaster, with Christmas looking at, and *for*, George and paying no attention to Linda. On Sunday, Linda told George to stay out of sight and urged me to sit at the ring getting Christmas's attention so her ears would stay up.

Our sweet girl's mostly black coat gleamed; her silver undercoat flashed through; her gorgeous tail fell into a saber, and her dark eyes sparkled in her ebony face. Linda took her in dead last, and it was a big class. They all went around together, and then each entry had an individual turn. When her moment finally came, Christmas's tan paws trotted close to the ground in perfect harmony, and she looked as though she had been showing forever. I sat next to Suzanne Kinman, who would go on to become a German Shepherd Dog judge. She whispered to me, "She's really nice!"

The judge moved her up to second place, and that's how it ended. It was just a red ribbon, but it meant the world to us. We had earned several blue ribbons with our other dogs, but only in "bred-by exhibitor" classes with no competition. The dog who beat Christmas became Reserve Winners bitch, second only to the female who won the show.

Despite the fact that she was never well after her emergency surgery, Christmas always remained fierce and joyful, and on that Sunday she looked exactly like the dog we had bred for--correct movement and conformation and showing perfect temperament for the judge. I could barely talk through my exultant tears, to thank Linda for her superb handling.

It was Christmas's last show. But on that one day, a respected judge had seen in our little pick of the litter what we had worked so hard to produce. On that one day, on Christmas's behalf, we were triumphant.

~*~

He may have roamed in his dreams, but Misha preferred to stay at home.

The Hike

A very nice lady in the local dog club invited members to go on a hike on her family farm. We brought picnic lunches and as many of our dogs as we wished. George and I decided to take Delta and Misha.

After Misha's miraculous response to the gold bead implants, when he began running we discovered he had bad elbows. They were bad enough that he needed surgery on one of them; we had him neutered at the same time.

The anesthesia was, as is standard, based on his weight, and Misha was still very skinny at seven months. We found out later that he awakened from anesthesia too soon, and it took several staff members to hold him down. Fortunately, the elbow surgery was a success. Misha, when fully recovered and not having some other medical crisis, ran circles around the "twins," as we called Alex and Bonnie since they were both solid black. He moved like a quarter horse, making very tight circles and quick turns, despite the fact that he was built more like a Thoroughbred--long and lean.

He loved for people to come to our house. He always thought they were visiting him! Besides, he adored being cuddled. He was useless as a watchdog. We joked about putting a sign on the door, "Burglars: please bring a dog." He and his littermates were all quite territorial about their property when it came to strange dogs, cats, and other critters. But all of them would have welcomed evil-doers in, and for a cookie would have showed them the silver.

Leaving home was a different story. But we thought he might enjoy going somewhere other than to a veterinarian. He and Delta got along well, and the farm was huge and far enough off the road that we could hike with the dogs off leash. The hike began perfectly--a group of happy dogs and owners, and a perfect spring day in Georgia. Misha seemed to be enjoying himself, and Delta definitely was, as she always did.

We got to a small pond, and Misha actually walked into it a short way, getting his paws wet. Suddenly, with no warning, he became hysterical and lunged for Delta, trying his best to bite her. He got George instead, who was between them, and who fortunately was wearing very thick pants which took the brunt of Misha's aggression. No skin was broken.

We were stunned. Misha had never before shown aggression toward Delta or toward any human being.

Our dear friends Dixie, Jerry, and Joye caught up to us, and we explained the situation and asked their advice. We were holding onto Misha for dear life, trying to keep him away from Delta because he was still acting crazed. He clearly did not recognize her.

Jerry very kindly drove his truck to our location, so we could load Misha into a portable crate. Joye's theory was that Misha had become over stimulated by all the dogs (they may have reminded him of the many times he had been at a vet's office for surgery, surrounded by strange dogs). We got him into our van and into his crate, and he stayed there, apparently quite content, while we continued to hike with Delta.

Misha eventually filled out and became a big, strong, beautiful German Shepherd Dog. But if we took him to a park, he hid under a bench. At the vet's waiting room, he trembled violently. It was heartbreaking.

Dr. John Wright, a renowned animal behaviorist, gave a seminar which Joye and I attended. I asked him about Misha, giving him a little background. He asked me if Misha had to go anywhere other than to the vet from time to time. I said no, and Dr. Wright's advice was to let Misha enjoy living his life at home, and not to make him go anywhere that he didn't have to. We took his advice and never regretted it.

His sisters acted as though they were afraid of him when he snarled at them (they weren't; Alex was the queen and everyone knew it; she once bit off the tip of his ear when he got a bit too impertinent). He sometimes stole her Kong toy, then looked at it as though to say, "What on earth does she see in this?" He had no play or toy drive of his own, he just enjoyed bedeviling Bonnie and Alex. We spoiled him rotten, and never again dragged him away from home unless it was absolutely necessary.

He was a very happy dog for the rest of his life.

~*~

Wolfsong in Georgia

Joye with Danny, the pups' half-brother, herding sheep.

Sheep!

As George turned into the long dirt driveway to Sandra Lindenmuth's sheep farm, Christmas, with me in the back seat of the van, sat up straight and focused ahead with laser-like intensity. For once, her mortal enemy Bonnie, crated in the van's cargo compartment, was forgotten. How could this be? Christmas had never seen, smelled, or known of a sheep before.

George and I were taking Christmas, Alexandra, and Bonnie for a Herding Instinct Test. After all, they were German *Shepherd* Dogs, and sheepherding was the breed's original purpose. But did that instinct still exist in young dogs who had lived pampered lives in suburbia? We were about to find out.

Bonnie, neurotic as always, forgot to confront Christmas (we kept them separated, just in case), and was most interested in 1) sheep poop, and 2) getting back into the van to head for the safety of home.

As we watched other members of the German Shepherd Dog Club of Atlanta go into a round pen with one dog and three sheep and do their best to follow Sandra's instructions, I could barely hold Christmas back. Finally, her turn arrived. Sandra's flock consisted of "hair sheep" who looked more like goats than sheep. They liked to run, and of course that piqued the interest of the dogs.

Because of the malabsorption disorder caused by the surgical removal of most of her intestines when she was nine weeks old, Christmas was unable to gain weight. Thus, she was a skinny, tiny, bony thing--but as I took off her leash and collar, she turned into a whirling dervish and leapt with her front legs and shoulders onto the back of the nearest sheep, biting furiously at its neck.

Sandra had assured us that nothing we or our dogs did would hurt the sheep, but I began to wonder. Sandra used her herding staff to tap Christmas on the back, trying to get her off the sheep. Christmas would get off one sheep and immediately attack the next one. She did not even feel the wood on her spine. She sported an incredibly huge grin on her little face--there was no other way to describe it--the entire time she was in the pen.

After what seemed an eternity but was probably only about 10 or 15 minutes, I asked Sandra to stop, fearing that the staff would hurt our pick of the litter puppy's unprotected backbone. Sandra did stop, and I called Christmas to me. She came immediately, although it was clear she had found her passion.

Next came Alexandra. I had seen her sire, Chimo's, herding instinct test at the German Shepherd Dog Club of America's national specialty (all GSD's) show a year or so previously. Alex's test was a virtual repeat of his. George took her in the ring, and she immediately began gently trotting around the sheep, changing directions whenever George asked her to, keeping the small flock together, collecting runaway sheep on her own, looking for all the world as though she knew this was what she had been born to do. Her huge, gorgeous solid black body was fluid and elegant as instinct took over. This time it was George who had the huge grin.

Finally it was Bonnie's turn. She made it clear she wanted to leave and had no interest whatsoever in herding sheep. Sandra was patient, but no go. We watched all the other participants work their dogs. Sandra graciously volunteered to put three lambs in the pen to see if they might awaken Bonnie's interest. At first no--but when Sandra literally dragged a lamb in front of Bonnie, the long-dormant instinct came to life, and lo and behold, there was our little "Bonnie Blue" trotting around the sheep, smiling!

All three puppies passed their herding instinct test. For Christmas, it was the very best day of her life.

We had not brought Misha, fearing that he might make a too-sharp turn and further damage his already vulnerable joints. He never had the pleasure of meeting sheep.

But Rajah and Delta did. Long before the puppies were born, I took Rajah to a herding clinic where the sheep were "woolies" and simply stood still in the ring. Rajah had better sense than to run around them like a Border Collie so he just stood there looking at me as though he were asking, "Mom, what do you want me to do? These sheep aren't moving and don't need to be herded."

The instructor told me to beat on the backs of the sheep to try to get them to move, so Rajah would be interested. You just haven't lived until you've been in the midst of a flock of sheep in a small pen and you are pounding on their backs with your fists, trying futilely to get them to move while you are desperately trying to keep from falling down when they push back. "Woolies" are a large, stupid breed. After we left the pen in disgrace, Rajah sat with me on the grass with his back to them.

At the herding instinct test at a National GSD show, Rajah showed tremendous interest and kept going after the wildest sheep of the bunch, but the judge flunked him for not keeping the sheep together! The test was supposed to be for instinct, not for a dog who was already trained to herd. Our friend Jerry saw the whole thing and said that Rajah had been cheated. I agreed.

Later, we took Rajah and Delta to Sandra's farm to try for the first time with her, and the third time with him. Although she bred and herded with Border Collies, Sandra did not expect German Shepherd Dogs to herd in the same fashion and had respect for their different methods. Rajah passed with flying colors and had a great time. Once, though, when a lamb lay down in front of him, Rajah also lay down, and Sandra said, "Oh, he won't hurt it."

George and I looked at each other, and George promptly went and got Rajah. Sandra didn't know that Rajah always ate lying down, and also didn't know about his hunting prowess.

Delta passed the herding instinct test as well, and for some months afterward we regularly took them on the long drive to Franklin, Georgia, to Sandra's farm. Once Delta got too enthusiastic, and we wound up having to hold a sheep while Sandra stitched it up. Rajah loved racing across the huge field after an errant sheep, but he was getting too old to take the heat and that much running. We never got any herding titles on any of our dogs, but watching our beloved shepherds prove the depths of the breed's untrained instinct gave us some of our happiest memories.

Wolfsong in Georgia

Alice Lovejoy Carnahan

Delta, ready to administer hugs to anyone who needed them.

Alice Lovejoy Carnahan

Tales from Tranquility

"Heaven?" the resident asked. She had been asleep when we entered her room at Tranquility, the local residential hospice I visited every Sunday with one of our registered therapy dogs. The first thing she saw when she opened her eyes was Alexandra, our beautiful, huge, solid black German Shepherd Dog. It turned out the resident once had a beloved GSD who looked just like Alex. Her dog had died years before, and she thought she was now in heaven with her old friend.

One week Delta and I entered a room full of visiting family and friends, and the resident, after introductions, sang "Delta Dawn" in perfect pitch, with all the right words.

On another Sunday I had just signed in when a nurse told me that the patient in Room 6 had just died, and some of his grandchildren might benefit from a therapy dog visit. Almost immediately, a beautiful little girl who appeared to be about three years old came up the hall crying. She stopped when she saw Delta, and I told her I was very sorry for her loss, and that Delta was there to give a hug to whoever needed one. She got down on her knees and threw her arms around Delta, but very gently. After obtaining permission, the little girl followed us as we made our rounds, never entering a private room but meeting us in the hall after each visit to get her "doggy hug." As I was preparing to leave, her slightly older sister saw us and thanked us for being such a blessing (her words) to her little sister. I said I was just glad that we happened to get there at exactly the time we did. The sister said, "Ma'am, that was no accident."

    Once, we walked by a common room and saw a couple who looked interested. We went in and explained that Alex was a therapy dog and was there for anyone who would like to pet or visit with her. The lady asked, "Is she a Golden?" and her husband explained that his wife was blind. She had had two guide dogs of her own but wasn't in a position to have one now. She really missed having her hands on a dog. Alex lay at her feet while the lady gently went over her whole body with hands. After a while she asked what her tail was like, and I moved Alex up so she could feel it. She said that must be why she thought she was a Golden-- she had such a nice coat. Those supplements were really working!

Years ago, I taught Delta to "speak" on command. So she could have entire conversations with everyone at Tranquility.

"Delta, say glad to meet you."
Woof!
"Say thank you."
Woof!
"Say it was great to see you."
Woof!
"Say yes! I am big and pretty and smart."
Woof! Woof!

The only problem: I never knew if her response would be barely audible or a full-throated German Shepherd roar. Once someone complimented me for training her to speak softly at the hospice. I just smiled.

During another visit, Delta burped in the hallway. A very nice nurse who had known her for months thought she was growling at her. I explained that Delta had never growled at a human being in her life. The nurse did not know that dogs burped!

Alex and I were in the hallway when a new patient was rolled in. The lady on the stretcher was awake--she sat up just a bit, saw Alex, and said, "beautiful dog." I like to think that this resident's first impression of Tranquility was a big, beautiful, smiling black dog with a purple kerchief around her neck.

A long-term resident and her husband became fast friends with both Delta and Alex. Ms. P. had a gorgeous sweet smile. Her husband always looked exhausted. They met when she was 15 years old and married when she was 20. He was 15 years older. He called her his "little princess." He fed her so well while she was at Tranquility that she gained 40 pounds! He rarely left her side. I felt so sorry for him, and yet I suspect that most couples do not come near what those two achieved in their time together.

Most hospice visits average 10 to 15 minutes apiece. I remember one day, however, when Delta and I visited in one room for more than an hour. Ms. L. was grieving the loss of her beloved Golden Retriever. She felt guilty for having left her Golden with someone else even though she herself was ill enough to enter the hospice. We cried together while Delta lay at her side. I told her the story about how dogs and their owners meet in heaven at the Rainbow Bridge. I'd brought Delta for the visit in response to a staff member who had asked me to visit that resident. Later, another volunteer told me it might be better if I did *not* take Delta to see Ms. L. since she had been attacked by a German Shepherd Dog in her childhood. Ironically, Delta had already provided much-needed solace to Ms. L. in regard to her own dog's death.

Ms. B. was thrilled to see Delta and made no bones about the fact that she related better to animals than people. She had a beloved cat named Baby Doll. I asked her what color Baby Doll was.

She said, "Black."

And I said, "I bet she's beautiful!"

Ms. B. replied without a blink, "Well, she's really smart!"

One resident told us she was okay with dogs if they didn't get too close to her, so I brought Alex in but kept her at least 10 feet away. Pretty soon, however, Ms. W. invited me to sit in a chair next to her recliner, and Alex sprawled comfortably at my feet--right next to her.

Ms. W. asked me to show her "what Alex can do," so we did some obedience exercises, heeling, etc. Ms. W.'s TV set was not working and she was waiting for someone to fix it. She told me that she had also asked for ice water and had not received any. I offered to go to the nursing station and pass on her requests, but she said no, she didn't get a visit from a dog very often and she'd like us to stay! Alex and I later saw the technicians who repaired her TV, and they made a point of telling me that Ms. W. had raved about her visit with the dog.

One day the petite cleaning lady who mopped the hospice floors, whom I had seen almost every Sunday for more than a year, asked, "Why do you bring your dog here?"

I told her that I brought the dogs to cheer up residents and their visitors.

She said, "Oh, to make them happy!"

I said yes, and she commented, "She's a very good dog." She was looking at Delta on a perfect down-stay, avidly watching the pocket where I kept her treats. She truly was the picture of devotion!

Once, a family member asked how we got started volunteering at Tranquility. I told her. The mother of my dear friend and coworker, Marion Striplin, had a massive stroke, and Marion was distraught at the thought of having to move her to a nursing home. Someone referred her to Tranquility, and her mother was admitted. I visited her and had never before seen such a gorgeous and peaceful place. Marion was immensely pleased with the care her mom was receiving. I asked the staff if they had pet therapy visitors. They did. I resolved to volunteer there as soon as I had another certified therapy dog; Rajah had died years previously. Delta and then Alexandra continued his legacy.

Marion became ill with pancreatic cancer. In December, 2006, she visited George and me at our home. She had visited many times before, and none of our dogs had ever jumped up on her or bothered her in any way. As soon as Marion got inside the door, Alex stood up and very gently placed her paws on Marion's chest. Alex refused to leave Marion's side during her entire visit. Marion died at Tranquility three weeks later.

I always thought that Delta and Alexandra's years of therapy dog work at the hospice were the best kind of tribute to her.

~*~

Alex and Bonnie.

Elbows

When many people hear "German Shepherd," they automatically think "hip dysplasia." That's a gross injustice, for two reasons. First, GSDs are now way down the list of breeds in terms of hip dysplasia prevalence. Second, it was German Shepherd Dog breeders who first recognized the hip problem, publicized their findings, and began the long, arduous road toward eradicating the condition. They did this by identifying affected animals and not breeding them. The Orthopedic Foundation for Animals (OFA) in the United States (there are similar organizations in other countries) owed its original existence to its ability to examine x-rays of dogs' hips and to judge whether or not the animal did or did not have hip dysplasia. Responsible breeders have been using OFA evaluations for years to help make wise breeding decisions, and it has paid off. German Shepherd Dogs are now, at the time of this writing, fortieth in prevalence of hip dysplasia of all breeds, according to the OFA's website, www.offa.org.

Thanks to the education George and I got from Joye and Dixie in conjunction with the German Shepherd Dog Club of Atlanta, we were determined to be the most responsible breeders possible. Delta passed all of her health screening tests with flying colors. Her intended, American Select Champion and Canadian champion Winning Ways Chimo, had even more health certifications than she did. The pups' pedigree was tremendously deep in dogs with good hips and elbows on both the sire and dam's sides.

But sometimes despite your best efforts nature kicks you in the teeth. There are several different problems that can occur with dogs' elbows. The worst is ununited anconeal process (UAP), in which two bones which should unite by age 20 to 24 weeks do not do so. I had heard of UAP and always thought that if a dog had it, he would be horribly lame and likely have to be put down. In Misha's case, he *was* terribly lame. After his gold bead implants enabled him to run despite his missing left hip socket, he developed extreme lameness in the front, and x-rays revealed a variety of problems in both of his elbows. How could that possibly be? The sling had pulled his left hip out of its socket, causing his hip dysplasia, but why would he have *elbow* dysplasia? No one in Delta's family had it, and Chimo had never previously produced it in any of the litters he had sired.

There was good news, however, for Misha: he had surgery and it was tremendously successful. We got Dr. Early to neuter him at the same time, since he would already be under general anesthesia. We didn't want Misha to accidentally breed one of his sisters.

Those sisters taught us more than we ever wanted to know about elbows. The Orthopedic Foundation for Animals will not assign a permanent hip or elbow rating to a dog under two years old. Shortly before Alexandra, Bonnie, and Christmas turned two, George noticed that Alex was toeing in with her left foot when she ran. We worried, but didn't have x-rays done as she was almost two, and we knew we would get them then.

Dr. Garrett in Roswell, Georgia, x-rayed Bonnie and Alexandra on the same day. Alex went first, and the condition showed clearly on the x-ray: a white line slicing through the middle of her elbow where no white line should be. Her left elbow had never united. Her other elbow was fine. Then Dr. Garrett came out with Bonnie's x-rays, and our beautiful little Bonnie Blue, who had never limped for a single second in her life, also had UAP on one side. Both Bonnie's and Alex's hip x-rays looked fine; the OFA rated Bonnie's as Good and Alex's as Fair, which is also a passing (non-dysplastic) grade.

Misha's elbow problems might have been a fluke. But three dogs in one litter was not a fluke: it was a genetic inheritance. We had hoped someday to breed Bonnie, who had excellent conformation and temperament. But we would breed her only if she passed all the tests her dam had aced. George and I made the responsible decision to have Alexandra and Bonnie spayed. We had not yet had Christmas x-rayed, but knew we would not be breeding her. The magnificent line that had begun with our friend Joye's Pebbles, continued through Dixie's Dakota and then through our beloved Delta would end with our litter. We would not take a chance of passing on damaged elbows to future generations.

We later had Christmas x-rayed, and all of her joints were perfect. OFA assigned a passing grade to her elbows and a Good rating to her hips.

Having read all this, by now you may be feeling terribly sorry for George and me and our dogs. Don't! Misha ran like a Thoroughbred racehorse for most of his life. Alex lived to be 10 ¾ years old and did develop spine problems possibly as a result of her altered gait, but for most of her life she was healthy, happy, and able to run without problems. And Bonnie, beautifully built little blue-black Bonnie, never limped a single day before she turned twelve.

And as our litter proved, even ununited elbows do not have to be a death sentence. We were careful, using ramps judiciously, not jumping Alex or Bonnie and giving appropriate supplements and medications, and their elbow problems didn't drastically change their lives.

Once again, responsible German Shepherd Dog breeders have recognized a problem and are and have been seriously interested in reducing the incidence of elbow problems. The OFA has seen a significant increase in submissions of elbow x-rays and of passing elbow evaluations, each year.

~*~

Bonnie Blue, mighty rabbit stalker.

Bunnies, or Dogs Will be Dogs

Close to bedtime on a wintry night George stomped in, furious after taking Alexandra out. He could barely look at her, and from the way she glared, the anger was mutual. Eventually the story emerged.

Alex was to have knee surgery the next day, so George had taken her to the lower paddock to do her business without interference from her dam and siblings. She was not supposed to run.

That's when an enormous rabbit made its last mistake: it popped up within Alex's hunting zone, and, pretending that she did not hear George's frustrated cries of "Come!" and "Leave it!" Alex galloped on three legs until she dispatched it with one final lunge. George eventually caught up to her, took the rabbit, or rather its *corpse*--the biggest wild rabbit he had ever seen--and threw it over the fence. Alex looked at him as though he had lost his mind, clearly communicating, "But it was *my* rabbit--I caught it fair and square. I deserved to keep it!"

Alex did have her surgery the next day, and she did well, but George and I always wondered if she might have done even better if she had never seen that rabbit.

There was a precedent. Not long after we adopted Rajah, our first GSD, who had been picked up from the streets where he scrounged his living, a small rabbit popped up right in front of him in our back yard. His hunting skills undiminished, Rajah immediately pounced on the poor little bunny and within seconds ate it in its entirety. George told me he knew he shouldn't punish Rajah, since he was just doing what came naturally. He did, however, brush Rajah's teeth.

Little Bonnie, who never disobeyed and always came when we called her, one night *didn't*. She had finally blossomed after outliving her dam and all of her siblings. Terrified that something awful had befallen her--she was old by then--I went looking for her in the back paddock. I soon found her, proudly dragging a rabbit carcass up the ramp. She finally dropped it on my repeated command, but she was clearly disappointed that she didn't get to present her gift to George. She was as happy and confident as I had ever seen her.

I never told Rajah's or Alex's "bunny stories" during their therapy dog visits.

Alice Lovejoy Carnahan

Nobody gives up on Christmas!

Teflon Dog

It was Labor Day morning when I went downstairs to feed Christmas and found her lying in a tiny heap gushing blood from both ends. I flew upstairs from the basement and yelled for George. With what seemed like superhuman strength, fueled by fear for her life, he carried her inert form up the stairs and into the van. We then raced toward the Cobb Veterinary Emergency Hospital.

Labor Day morning meant the running of the annual Cobb County mini-marathon, and it took place very near our route. George took that into account as we ran every red light. We came out just above the race and just below the hospital.

I ran inside and told the receptionist my dog was dying, and I thought she had HGE. Techs brought out a stretcher and wheeled her back to the emergency intake area. She had been not quite right the night before, and we had brought her in then (it was a Sunday). She had had preemptive IV fluids, as the vet on call couldn't pinpoint anything definitely wrong with her. But we knew our girl: something was wrong.

HGE stands for hemorrhagic gastroenteritis. It's a disease which causes internal and sometimes external bleeding. We knew about it because Christmas's great-uncle had had it as a young dog. No one knows what causes it. The treatment is antibiotics, blood transfusions as needed, and fluids. It can be a killer, but it is possible for dogs to recover from it completely.

We left our little girl in the capable and caring hands of the emergency hospital personnel. They let me go back to see her after they had her hooked up to IV's. Joye told me the next day that meant that they didn't think she would make it.

Meanwhile, our other four German Shepherd Dogs needed to be fed and cared for. On Tuesday I had to return to work. We prayed for Christmas, who had already been through so much.

Although surgery had saved her life after her intussusception, the subsequent bacterial infection never left her, and she was never well. She could not absorb food no matter how much she ate, and she looked something like one of those poor starving children from Biafra. She herself, however, never acknowledged that she was sick, and she never lost her fierce and competitive spirit.

While Christmas fought for her life at the emergency clinic, I thought about her last crisis, when she was spayed. She had excellent conformation, and a couple of years previously we had considered entering her in a special conformation class at the German Shepherd Club of America's national specialty show. It was for dogs who had hips and elbows certified by the Orthopedic Foundation for Animals. In conformation shows in the United States (such as the famous Westminster Dog Show), because they are supposed to be showcases for breeding stock, only unspayed or unneutered dogs may compete. We later changed our mind about entering her in the show and decided to go ahead and get her spayed. We certainly were not going to breed her.

Dr. Phillip King, our terrific primary veterinarian, agreed to spay her, and did. When we arrived at his office to pick her up and bring her home, he decided to check her one last time. He found some bleeding through her bandage, and wasn't alarmed but of course checked more thoroughly. She was bleeding internally, a very bad sign. Julie Burgess, his wonderful vet tech, told us later that the two of them worked on her through the evening and she had rarely seen Dr. King look so grim. He was fully aware of what we--and more importantly, our dogs--had been through, and he was absolutely determined not to lose Christmas. We never knew what caused the problem, but our guess was that after-effects of the extensive life-saving surgery she had had as a puppy likely contributed. She never had problems from the spay surgery after that.

Now here she was, once again flirting with disaster and enduring intensive treatment for HGE. We visited her often, which staff there encouraged, and desperately tried to get her to eat. She wasn't interested. She stayed on IV fluids for a long time.

Finally, the vets decided that she no longer was in danger of dying, and since she was depressed and not really getting better, she might as well go home. They said just to try to keep her somewhat quiet.

We brought her home, and she ran into the house with a look of sheer glee on her little dark face. The first thing she did was run to our bedroom and leap upon the bed. Christmas was back!

~*~

Wolfsong in Georgia

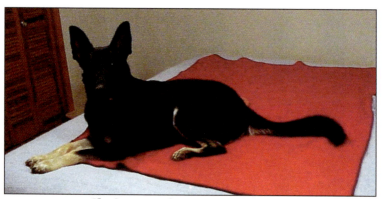

Christmas, home and happy.

Miraculous Red Liquid

Christmas may have been a Teflon dog, but she still had no appetite and looked as though she had anorexia. After her intussusception, she had developed a bacterial overgrowth and a malabsorption disorder. She could eat when she chose to but rarely did, and the calories didn't stick. She had chronic, lifelong diarrhea, although she was continent. It was no wonder she would rather play with her Kong toy than eat anything, even the choicest delicacy.

In the fall of 2001, I became so frustrated by her condition that I began searching the web for anything that might help. In addition to all of her other problems, she had a cobalamin deficiency. Cobalamin is Vitamin B12. However, she had had many B12 shots, and none of them had done her any good.

My search turned up Dr. John Fyfe, a researcher at Michigan State University. I sent him an email outlining the basics of Christmas's history and current treatment. The very next day he replied!

He pooh-pooh'ed the idea of any alternative veterinary treatments, and said that we should stick with just one vet. More important, he said that he had once adopted a dog with a problem that sounded very similar to Christmas's. He began treating his puppy weekly with a liquid form of cobalamin, given subcutaneously (just under the skin)--and the pup began gaining weight. He described the liquid as "the most beautiful red color you will ever see," and said it was inexpensive and could be bought at many feed stores, as it was usually given to livestock.

George and I took a copy of Dr. Fyfe's email to Dr. King, who is extremely competent himself but is never afraid to try new ideas. We asked him if he would order the liquid and give it to Christmas once a week. He agreed.

Within ten days of getting her first injection, Christmas regained a normal appetite. We no longer had to beg her to eat. That was the first time she had enjoyed food since she was nine weeks old. Now she was three and a half! She began to gain weight.

Within a year, she put on 30 pounds and thrived during all of 2002.

Dr. Fyfe had given Christmas one glorious good year of life.

Christmas, our fierce angel.

Dog Friends

Even a Teflon dog can't live forever. One morning when I took Christmas out before leaving for work, she got tired after I threw her beloved Kong saucer just a few times. That had never happened before. And her poop was tarry black. I called George from work and asked him to take her to our vet. He did, and Dr. King immediately started her on an IV and referred her to Georgia Veterinary Specialists (GVS), a premier emergency and specialty veterinary hospital in Sandy Springs just north of Atlanta. She was a couple months short of her fifth birthday. Despite all of her medical problems, she rarely acted sick, and gamely competed in agility trials, roaring at passing Rottweilers.

We visited her at GVS as often as we could. Once we took George's dad, "Mr. C," who adored all of our dogs. That day she seemed to perk up a bit, and actually played with one of the Kong toys we took for her. Another time we took Delta, her mother, to see her. Christmas didn't seem to care.

She was there for eleven agonizingly long days. They did scopes and tried all kinds of different treatments. Nothing made any difference. I kept our friends updated with frequent emails. I remember being thrilled when we found out that Christmas did not have cancer. I should have realized that cancer is not the only killer.

Dr. Dorfman, our favorite internal medicine vet at GVS, eventually called and said he was very sorry, but they had done everything they knew to do, and he felt we should let Christmas go. Through our tears, we agreed and scheduled to go in on Saturday morning.

We got to GVS on a beautiful, sunny February day. As we were waiting for Christmas to be brought to us and for Dr. Dorfman to arrive, Dixie and Jerry showed up. Then Joye came. Then Judith and Armando Aguilar. We had met them, too, through the German Shepherd Dog Club of Atlanta, and like Dixie, Jerry, and Joye, they became lifelong friends. We had not asked for any of them to come--they just did. Dr. Dorfman came in and seemed rather inappropriately cheerful, and Joye said, "Do you know why we're here?" He said he did, but he thought maybe there was a chance that Christmas might get better if we gave her a little more time. And he suggested that we take her outside on a rolling cart, so she could enjoy the Georgia winter sunshine. We did, and had a lovely visit with our "dog friends" and our beloved, feisty little bicolor dog who didn't know she was sick and thought she had to protect us from all other dogs.

When we left, we took our friends to lunch at a nearby restaurant. They seemed cheered, but I was not. I knew our little girl too well.

The next morning Dr. Dorfman called and said he felt horrible, but Christmas had gone into respiratory distress, and we needed to come and say goodbye. We agreed, and did. It was the only thing to do when we saw her little head bobbing uncontrollably, even while she was hooked up to a myriad of IV lines.

We brought her home in a cardboard coffin GVS provided. George buried her in the back yard in the cold, pouring rain. She had made it almost five years on sheer, indomitable willpower. We still miss her, and will for the rest of our lives.

But losing her taught us once again that there are no better friends than dog friends.

We will always be grateful to Dixie, Jerry, Joye, Judith, and Armando for coming to be with us in our grief, and then helping us enjoy one last sunny outing with our beloved little dog.

Wolfsong in Georgia

Misha loved to be massaged.

Neurosurgery

"Misha collapsed and he can't get up!"

George's frantic call interrupted my work day and sent chills of fear coursing through me. Poor little Misha; he'd already been through so much. What could be wrong now? We agreed that George would get him to the vet. He did, somehow managing to heave Misha's 85-pound body into the car. Dr. King diagnosed a spine problem and referred Misha to GVS. Misha was seven years old. At that time there were very few veterinary neurologists/neurosurgeons in Georgia. GVS had one.

Dr. Ronald Johnson evaluated Misha shortly after his arrival. Misha had an injured disc and would require surgery. We agreed, and he came through the surgery splendidly. His operation was very similar to the kind undergone by a human being who had "blown a disc."

Our phone rang at 1:00 a.m. on the night after the surgery. Was it bad news? Julie, the vet tech who loved all our dogs, had gone on vacation to Hawaii. Her plane had just landed, and she called to ask how Misha was doing. We were thrilled to tell her that Dr. Johnson was very pleased with the results. We were awed by the fact that Julie took time out from a rare Hawaii vacation to check on our little man.

There was just one problem: when Misha was discharged, he still couldn't get up and walk on his own.

We began the long process of helping him up and then taking him for short walks outside. George set up a bed in the dining room, and he and Misha stayed there day and night. Once Misha was up with the assistance of gentle support under the base of his tail or a sling-type harness, he walked so fast he was almost trotting. And he was always very cooperative about pooping and peeing on a leash. His spirits were excellent; he was unfazed by his inability to get up on his own. George, however, was tied to the house and could only leave for short periods of time, since Misha was unable to use the dog door to get outside.

Before this incident, Misha had benefitted from canine massage. In fact, he adored it. Jeanie Ward, a certified massage therapist (for people) had switched to canine massage at the urging of a holistic veterinarian, some years before. Jeanie had come to our house many times to give massages to all of our dogs. Misha was probably the most appreciative canine client she ever had. He would wriggle with pleasure, sprawled on his huge couch-shaped orthopedic dog bed, while her skilled hands relieved all the tension in his damaged body.

Weeks after his surgery, we were beginning to despair that Misha would ever be able to get up on his own. Jeanie made a special trip just for him. As always, he adored the attention and the wonderful sensation of her loving touch.

Two days later, Misha got up on his own. He ran for the next three years.

Alexandra memorialized in stained glass.

The Gift

You are not supposed to have favorites among your children, and you are not supposed to have favorites among the puppies you have bred and kept. But there was no doubt that Alexandra was the love of George's life.

She died of bleeding ulcers in December of 2008 at age ten and three quarters, after a neurologist put her on steroids to try to alleviate her mobility problems.

We had taken her off her Deramaxx, a non-steroidal anti-inflammatory medication, for the prescribed amount of time before beginning the steroids, but it was obviously too soon for her system. Earlier in her life, we had given her a very mild sedative for severe thunderstorm anxiety, and it seemed to help. But the last time we gave her just a half dose of the same medication she went into a coma and we thought we had killed her. Something about her body could not handle medication in normal doses.

Because of that, when she developed neurological symptoms, we had declined to put her through diagnostic tests which required general anesthesia. She had developed some type of spinal problem in the fall of 2008, and she lurched about painfully. So we took her to the veterinary neurologist at GVS.

I had retired Alex from therapy dog work due to her labored gait several months before we took her to Dr. Johnson, who had performed Misha's surgery. Shortly after we started the steroids, we awakened to find her coughing up blood. She was too weak to get up and walk on her own.

George managed to lift her and get her into the car, and we rushed her to Dr. King. He recommended that we take her straight to GVS while he called and made the referral. The GVS vets confirmed the diagnosis of bleeding ulcers and said that only emergency surgery could save her life. She made it through the surgery, but died peacefully in her sleep the night after.

We miss her, as we miss all of our pups, every day of our lives. But it's worse for George. He started out disliking her because as a pup she was mean to all of her littermates.

She was born an alpha bitch, and she died one. But along with her dominance came an inherent confidence that exuded from her every pore. As an adult, she never felt the need to demonstrate her lofty status; it simply was. Her brilliance and intelligence shone from her dark eyes, and it was not unusual for strangers who met her to say, "She's really smart, isn't she?"

When Delta, Alexandra, Bonnie, and Misha were all still living and doing well, we asked our friend Joyce Quick to come to our house and take photographs of us and them. We had met Joyce through the dog club, and she had begun taking professional photos at dog shows. She took many, many pictures, and we bought all of the best ones. But one stood out: a magnificent head shot of Alexandra. Joyce had taken it in front of our chain-link fence, but had edited out the fence and left only Alexandra's alert ears, stunning solid black head, intelligent eyes, and just slightly graying muzzle. Joyce's photograph of Alexandra is on the cover of this memoir. After Alex died, I had a locket made with that photo engraved inside. George wears it every day.

In the fall of 2010, I began thinking of what I could give to George for Christmas. We had talked for years about wanting a stained glass German Shepherd, but had never found one that we liked. One night I began surfing the web trying to find someone who could create a custom stained glass portrait based on Alex's gorgeous head shot. I found many artists who did custom work at astronomical prices, and I didn't even like their pictures. And then I found Stained Glass Pets. The artist's name was Kevyn Cundiff, so naturally I assumed the artist was male, which turned out not to be the case. (I made out the deposit check to Mr. Kevyn Cundiff after which she politely corrected me.)

Her pet portraits were jaunty and somewhat comical, but there was something about her art that appealed to me, and I thought she could do a serious dog portrait if asked. One of her paintings, not of a dog at all, was called "Afterglow" and showed the backs of Adirondack chairs with empty wine glasses sitting on their ledges. One of the chairs was the most beautiful clear red color I had ever seen.

I emailed Kevyn and told her what I had in mind, which was a 9" diameter portrait of Alex. Her price was so reasonable that I asked her to tell me what a 14" diameter portrait would cost. She did, and we emailed back and forth what seemed to be a million times. She would send a sketch; I would reply with feedback; back would come the next one, usually the very next day. She never once lost patience.

Finally the head was just right, and it was time to choose the background. I chose a very simple background of horizontal color bands, so that it would not distract from Alex's portrait. The bottom was the claret red from the "Afterglow" painting, and the top a band of clear blue. Those colors went perfectly with the two smaller stained glass pieces which would hang on either side of the portrait, as well as with our living room and the red Oriental rug which graces it.

Finally we agreed it was done, and Kevyn shipped it. I could not bear to wait, and made George open it on the spot when it arrived a few days after Thanksgiving.

Alexandra's portrait now presides regally over our living room, and as for George, he said it was the best present he had ever received.

~*~

Misha, a study in courage.

Stem Cell Therapy

Misha's life was a catalog of what could go wrong with a dog.

Born with no sac and not breathing, with a luxated patella which was first misdiagnosed and then initially treated with a sling which pulled his left hip out of its socket; he had endured gold bead implants, elbow surgery, a ruptured cruciate ligament which required surgery, neurosurgery on his spine, and leptospirosis. It's no wonder that he never wanted to leave home!

Yet through it all, he remained a cuddly teddy bear, welcoming all and sundry to his home and thrilling to the touch of anyone who got near him. Hardly anyone could resist him. He was the only German Shepherd Dog I ever knew who was both cute and beautiful all at the same time.

And he ran. Oh, how he ran! That was probably his saving grace. He developed immense muscle in place of his nonexistent left hip socket. He had two bad elbows and one bad hip. And yet he persevered. Until one morning in his older age, he just couldn't any more.

He was no longer able to use his rear legs. But his eyes were bright and shiny with life, and we were not ready to give up on him. We had heard of a brand new treatment that was reputed to help almost any medical condition. Dr. King did tons of research, and so did I. He found that the University of Georgia did stem cell treatment, but only on dogs which were completely healthy except for the condition the stem cell treatment was supposed to help.

There was no way we could claim "complete health" for Misha. Despite having been vaccinated for it, Misha had developed leptospirosis a few years earlier; I later read that large-breed male dogs with deep chests seem particularly susceptible to it. There are many different strains or serovars, and vaccines (at least at that time) for only some of them. He had had all the vaccines available. He got lepto anyway, and it was only thanks to Dr. King's prompt treatment and, once again, the services of GVS, that he survived. But it damaged his liver and kidneys. Even so, by the time we decided on a vet who did stem cell therapy in the metro Atlanta area, and she did a complete blood analysis on him as part of the pre-operative workup, his results were completely normal.

Dr. Michelle Dickler in Snellville, Georgia, is a kind and competent vet who treated Misha, Bonnie (who always went along; by that time only she and Misha were left in our little Wolfsong family), George and me with compassion and respect. She even came out to the van to give the stem cell injections to Misha.

We took him in on a Monday. She put him under general anesthesia and harvested fat cells from behind his elbow. Then we took him home, and she shipped the fat cells in a special container to a company in California which worked its magic and returned them as stem cells. On Wednesday we took Misha back, and she injected the stem cells into his non-existent left hip socket.

The anesthesia apparently caused his previously damaged kidneys to fail once again. At the four-week checkup, Dr. Dickler found more muscle mass at the site of the stem cell injections to the left hip than she did on his (good) right hip. But it was not enough to overcome the ruined kidneys.

George heroically gave Misha IV fluids twice a day, for months. Misha's eyes were still shiny, and his mind seemed good, but he would not eat on his own. He seemed happy for us to take him out, but could not get up on his own. Once we got outside and supported his rear, he could walk (pretty fast!), pee, and poop. Then we would bring him back inside and settle him onto one of his huge orthopedic beds; we had one in the dining room and one in the living room. Once he was there, he couldn't get off unless we helped him. We took him out and turned him frequently, to prevent bedsores. He never got one.

One day we took him outside, and his front end collapsed. I just said "George," and he nodded. I called Dr. King, who very kindly came to our home. Misha was just as glad to see him as he always was with any visitors. George and I felt like murderers.

Julie later told us that Dr. King thought we had actually waited way too long, but we would have felt even worse if we hadn't tried everything we could. And Misha, I truly believe, was a happy dog right up to and through the end.

~*~

Wolfsong in Georgia

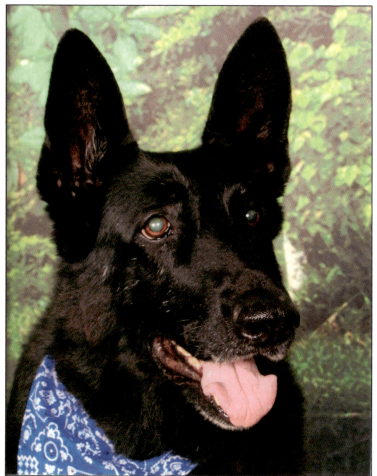

Our beautiful Bonnie Blue.

Explosion!

"Bonnie's not right." The dog sitter's opinion was borne out by Bonnie herself: listless and with no appetite at all. We had left Bonnie at our house with Cathy, whom she knew and liked, while we attended a wedding out of town. Bonnie had turned twelve on April 2, and now it was the end of the month. We had to get Cathy, who didn't drive, back to the pickup point for her Sunday night drive home. George took her and I stayed home with Bonnie, who was indisputably ill.

On Monday morning we took Bonnie to the vet. She was given fluids. Her blood levels were skewed; she needed to have an ultrasound.

Dr. Lindsay Boozer, an internal medicine vet, could not see her before Wednesday. We nursed Bonnie at home until then. Dr. Boozer did the ultrasound and told us, "Bonnie's gallbladder has exploded, and her only chance is to go directly to surgery."

Dr. Thomas Noone was operating on a Jack Russell Terrier who had swallowed a foreign object and was touch and go. Dr. Boozer interrupted him to explain Bonnie's situation, and he said of course he would operate on her. He was supposed to have Wednesday afternoon off.

He didn't get *that* one.

Dr. Noone removed Bonnie's gallbladder, spleen, and part of her liver. No one thought she would make it through the surgery, but she did. She stayed several days with Dr. Boozer and her wonderful staff, and finally we were able to bring her home. Dr. Noone and Dr. Boozer both gently tried to let us know that she might not make a full recovery.

But she fooled us all. At her follow up visits, her blood work looked so good that Dr. Boozer would redo it. On all of her visits, Bonnie had "the blood work of a two-year old."

We took all the advice that Dr. Boozer and Dr. Noone gave us, and Bonnie was a happy camper. Soon she was back to her old self. And we found out that the little terrier survived his surgery, too.

~*~

Wolfsong in Georgia

Bonnie, last of the litter.

Last Dog Standing

Today, August 2, Bonnie turned 13 years and four months old. She has outlived all the others. If she were human, she would be over 100.

After Misha, her last littermate, died we thought that since she had never lived without another dog, we might have to run out and get her one.

We were beyond wrong.

Born neurotic, desperately wanting to be alpha but not hardwired for it, Bonnie had spent her entire life seeking attention in any form. When we bought a machine which emitted high-frequency sound uncomfortable to dogs to stop the puppies' barking, it worked for all of them except Bonnie: she barked to set it off. Same with the citronella anti-bark collar.

Now she blossomed, clearly indicating, "I'm finally the Queen, the boss, the alpha! It sure took you long enough to get rid of all the others. This is finally *my* time!"

She had a few really good months after the gallbladder surgery before she began gradually losing the use of her rear end. She has degenerative myelopathy, a spinal disease that is the bane of many older German Shepherd Dogs. It is progressive and fatal; the one blessing is that it is also painless. Many years earlier, we had lost Rajah to it without knowing what it was.

Bonnie can still, most of the time, manage the one step into our sunken living room. She can usually manage the two steps into the sunroom and the dining room/library. When she does fall, generally she gets herself up before we can get to her. She still does her best to herd us together. We are her pack. But a few times she has fallen with her rear legs splayed out like a frog's and has been unable to arise without assistance.

It is terrifying: what if we were not home to help? Most of the time she can still navigate our long ramp to the back paddock, although she collapses occasionally. She gets herself back up and trudges on. On good days we take her to the front yard where she marks as much as possible, as if saying, "This is my home and don't you forget it!" She remains merry, oblivious to the disease that is slowly but inexorably draining her life away.

On a Sunday evening two weeks after I wrote this, Bonnie had a stroke, became disoriented and blind and lost the quintessential brightness that defined her. We took her to Dr. King the next morning and made the decision to let her go.

She was thirteen years, four and a half months old. Her last two years were her happiest.

The Orthopedic Foundation for Animals now has a DNA saliva test to screen for the mutated gene that has been seen in dogs with degenerative myelopathy. Now that a test is available, it should be possible to breed out that dreaded disease in dog breeds with a high preponderance of DM.

Alice Lovejoy Carnahan

Delta with friend.

Afterword

My editor said I should not end this "dogoir" on a sad note, and I agree.

The love and joy that Delta, Christmas, Alexandra, Misha and Bonnie brought us far outweighed the heartbreak of their--and Oscar's--tragedies. I hope that I have managed to convey a bit of their incredible personalities: Delta's constant cheer; our fierce angel Christmas's undiluted *joie de vivre;* Misha's unending courage, mischief and joy throughout a life that almost wasn't; Alexandra's nobility (she truly was Alexandra Danilova, Princess of all the Russias); and Bonnie's sweetness.

Would we have done this breeding if we had had foresight of what was to come? Of course not!

But then we would have never known the magnificent German Shepherd Dogs who made our life so much more than it would have been had they never existed.

After Bonnie's death, George and I decided we would wait two and a half years to get our next dog. That would give us time to get our finances in order and do some traveling.

When we told them our plans our friends doubled over with laughter.

What do you think?

You'll have to wait for **Wolfsong's Last Chapter**.

About the Author

Neither George nor I grew up as "dog people." We met when I was assigned to help him with an unwieldy caseload at the Macon, Georgia, Vocational Rehabilitation office where we both worked as counselors. Serendipitously, we lived in the same apartment complex. After work we would frequently meet a neighbor and his adorable West Highland White Terrier. Mr. Napier would put the dog on top of the stone wall to watch the rush hour traffic. We had never seen a Westie before, but were enchanted with the little fellow's looks and personality.

A few years later, we were newlyweds living in Thomasville, Georgia, 30 miles north of Tallahassee, Florida and met Annette, who owned, bred, and showed Westies. We became friends, and one day she came to our home and said, "I have a Westie for you!" Longtime Westie breeder Helen Craigmiles had a three year old male Westie champion who did not get along with her other male. We could have him if we agreed to allow him occasionally to be bred to one of her female Westies. We met him and fell in love. He was our only dog for the next twelve years. Not long after he joined our family, we fell into (pun intended) foxhunting and added horses to our family, too.

I had majored in journalism, but my best grade was for an obituary, and I didn't have the killer instinct for investigative reporting. I switched to public relations but hated it. I worked in various counseling and human services jobs for many years. George adores history, and he's an artist. I am addicted to reading murder mysteries. But our joint passion is animals. At the Thomasville library, a book title caught my eye: **How to be Your Dog's Best Friend.** It opened my mind to the possibility of living with dogs in a different way than I had ever imagined. It was published by the Monks of New Skete. I had no idea that someday I would own German Shepherd Dogs descended from one bred by Helen "Scootie" Sherlock, who helped the monks set up their breeding program.

Karma?

~*~

For more information

Should you be interested in learning more about GSDs and/or the organizations which promote them, their health, or well-being, the links below will provide a great start. All were active at the time of publication.

An amazing video tribute to GSDs -- http://www.youtube.com/watch?v=7dwYca6rONA&sns=fb

German Shepherd Dog Club of America -- www.gsdca.org

German Shepherd Dog Club of America -- Working Dog Association, Inc. – www.gsdca-wda.org

American German Shepherd Dog Charitable Foundation -- www.agsdcf.org (This one is very dear to my heart because it funds health research for GSD's. 10% of profits from this book will be donated to the AGSDCF.)

American German Shepherd Rescue Association – www.agsra.com

Military Working Dog Team Support Association – www.mwdtsa.org

Alice Lovejoy Carnahan

Photo credits

We're delighted so many of our friends have offered their support and encouragement for this book. Not only that, many graciously agreed to let us use some of their photographs. We want to acknowledge each of them.

Pg viii: Pebbles. Photo by Dixie Whitman

Pg viii: Dakota. Photo by Dixie Whitman

Pg 6: Rajah. Photo by Dixie Whitman

Pg 60: Santa and infamous ear. Photo courtesy of the Atlanta Humane Society

Pg 74: Herding sheep. Photo by Dixie Whitman

Pg 82: Delta. Photo by Dixie Whitman

Pg 90: Alex and Bonnie. Photo by Joyce Quick

Pg 110: Christmas. Photo by Tien Tran

Pg 116: Misha. Photo by Joyce Quick

Pg 132: Bonnie. Photo by Hollywood Pets

Pg 140: Delta & friend. Photo by Dixie Whitman

Wolfsong in Georgia

Alice Lovejoy Carnahan

- PQ
24.99
3.00

636.7
CA

DATE DUE

PRINTED IN U.S.A.

Made in the USA
Lexington, KY
12 November 2013